Big Words for Little Experts

Dinosaurs

Written by Fran Bromage
Consultant Emma Ranade
Illustrated by Ela Smietanka and Ana Gomez

Miles Kelly

Caudipteryx
feathers
For help pronouncing the dinosaur names, turn to the back of this book.
Allosaurus
razor-sharp teeth

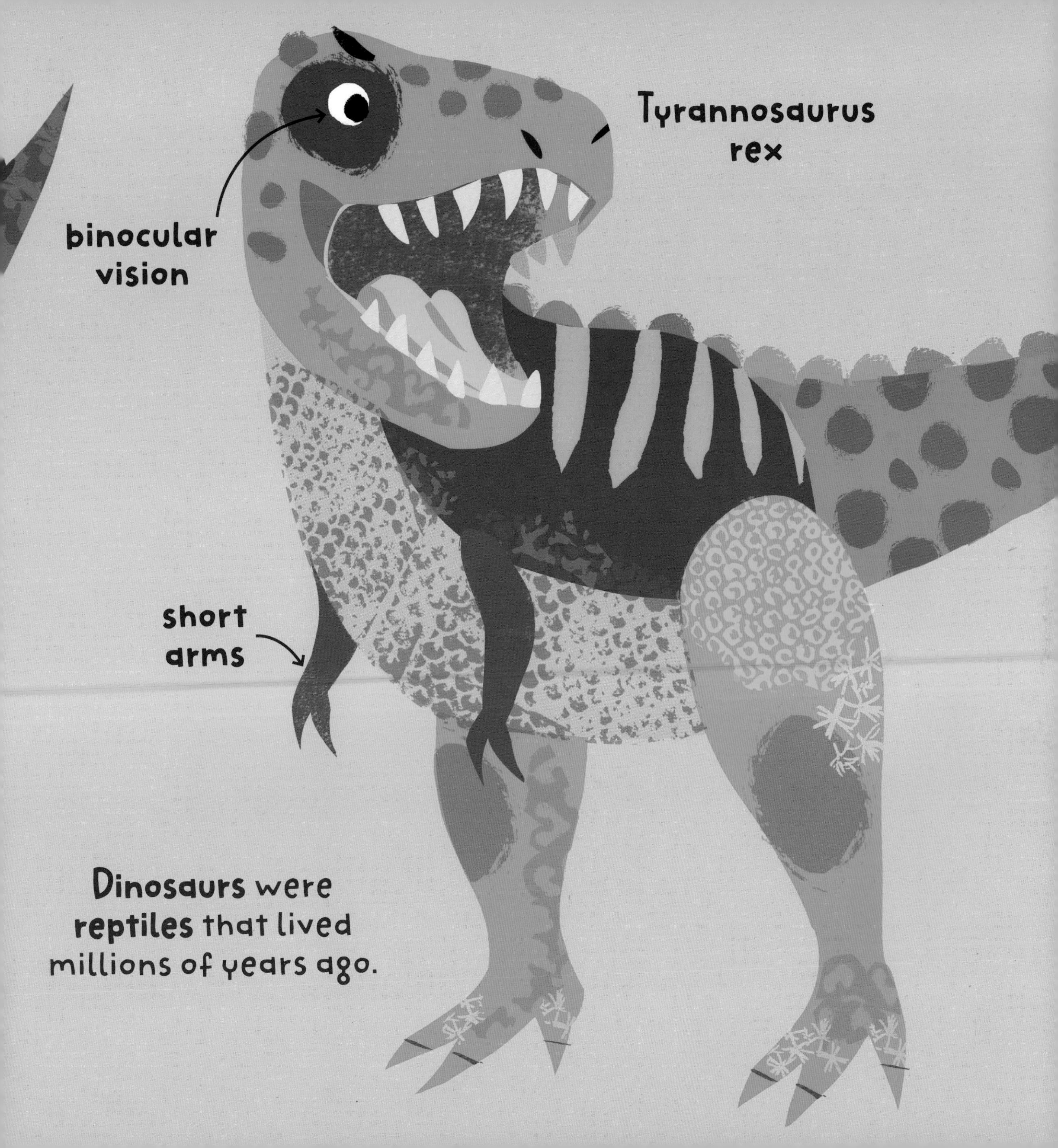

Dinosaurs were **reptiles** that lived millions of years ago.

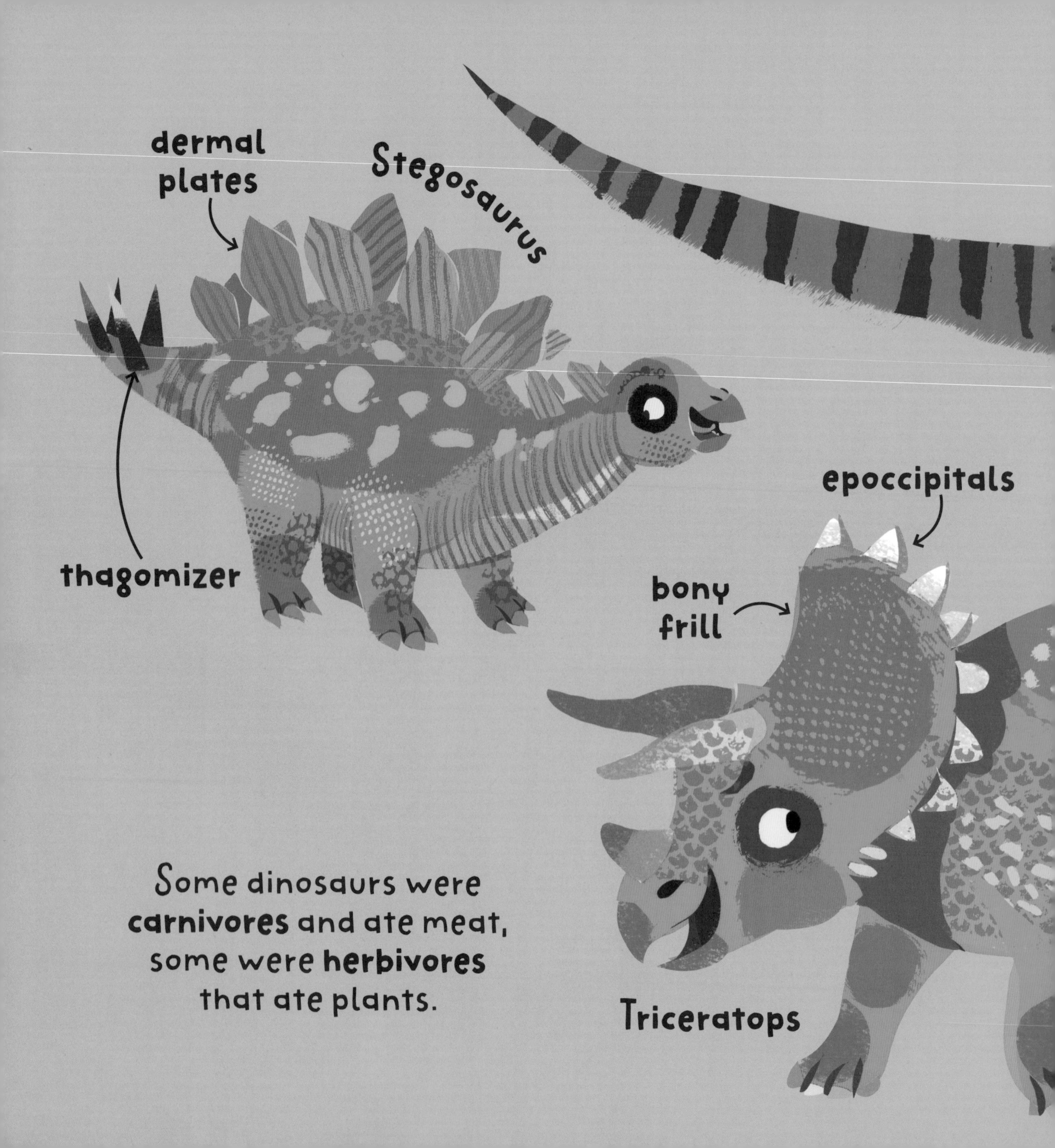

Some dinosaurs were **carnivores** and ate meat, some were **herbivores** that ate plants.

Apatosaurus
Nigersaurus
chisel-shaped
teeth

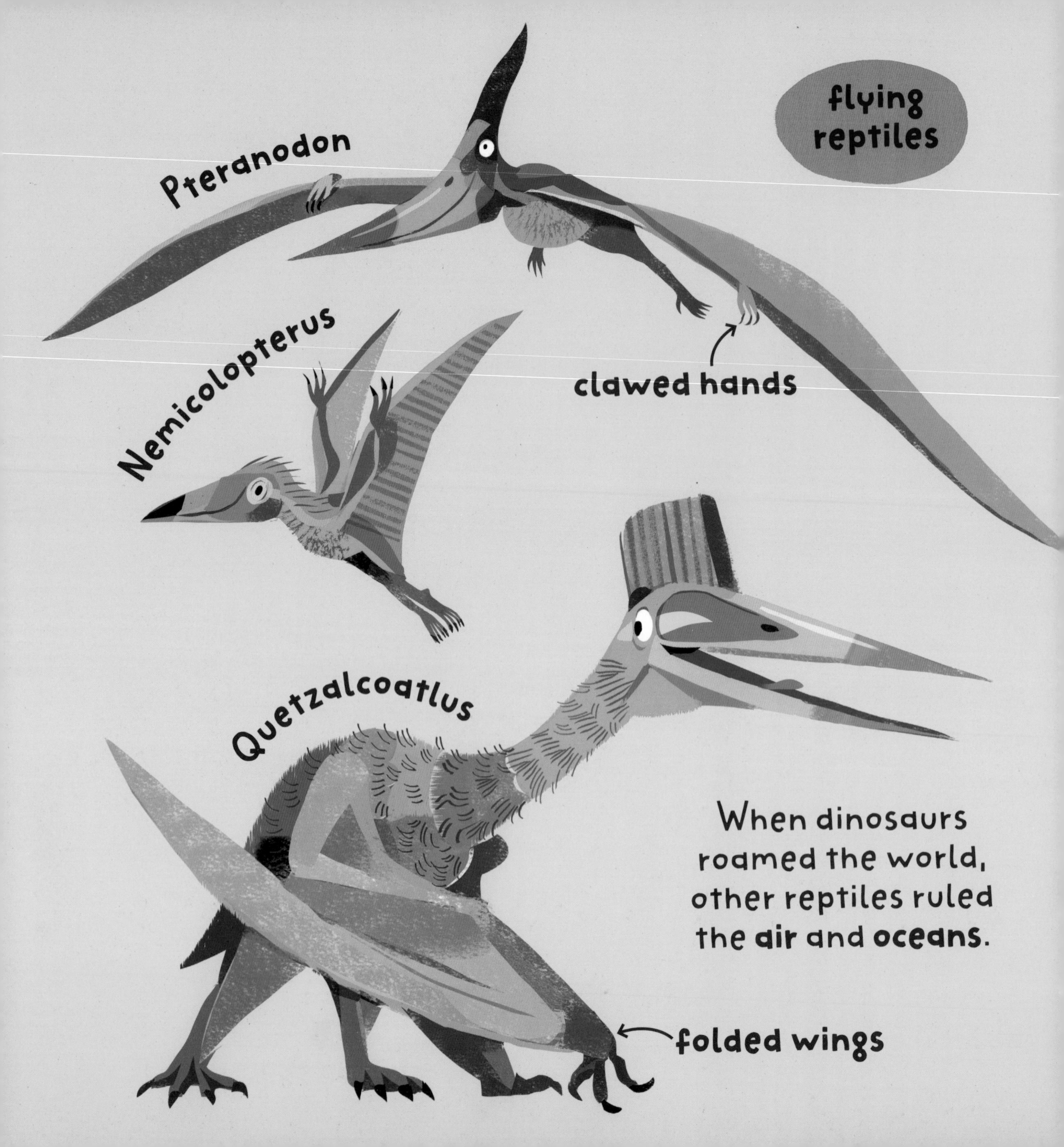

When dinosaurs roamed the world, other reptiles ruled the **air** and **oceans**.

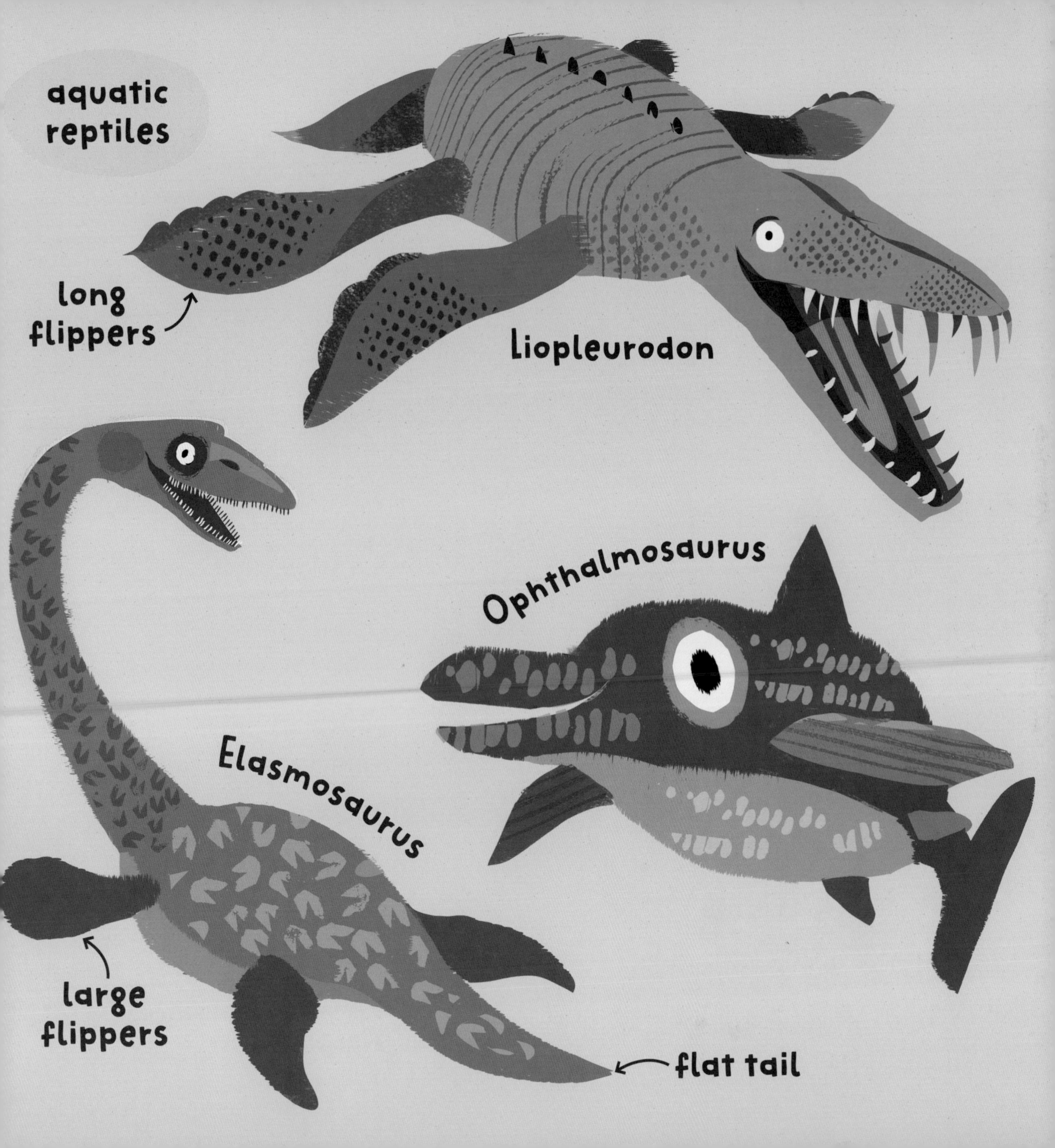
aquatic reptiles
long flippers
Liopleurodon
Ophthalmosaurus
Elasmosaurus
large flippers
flat tail

Dinosaurs came in all **shapes** and **sizes** with spikes, crests and claws.

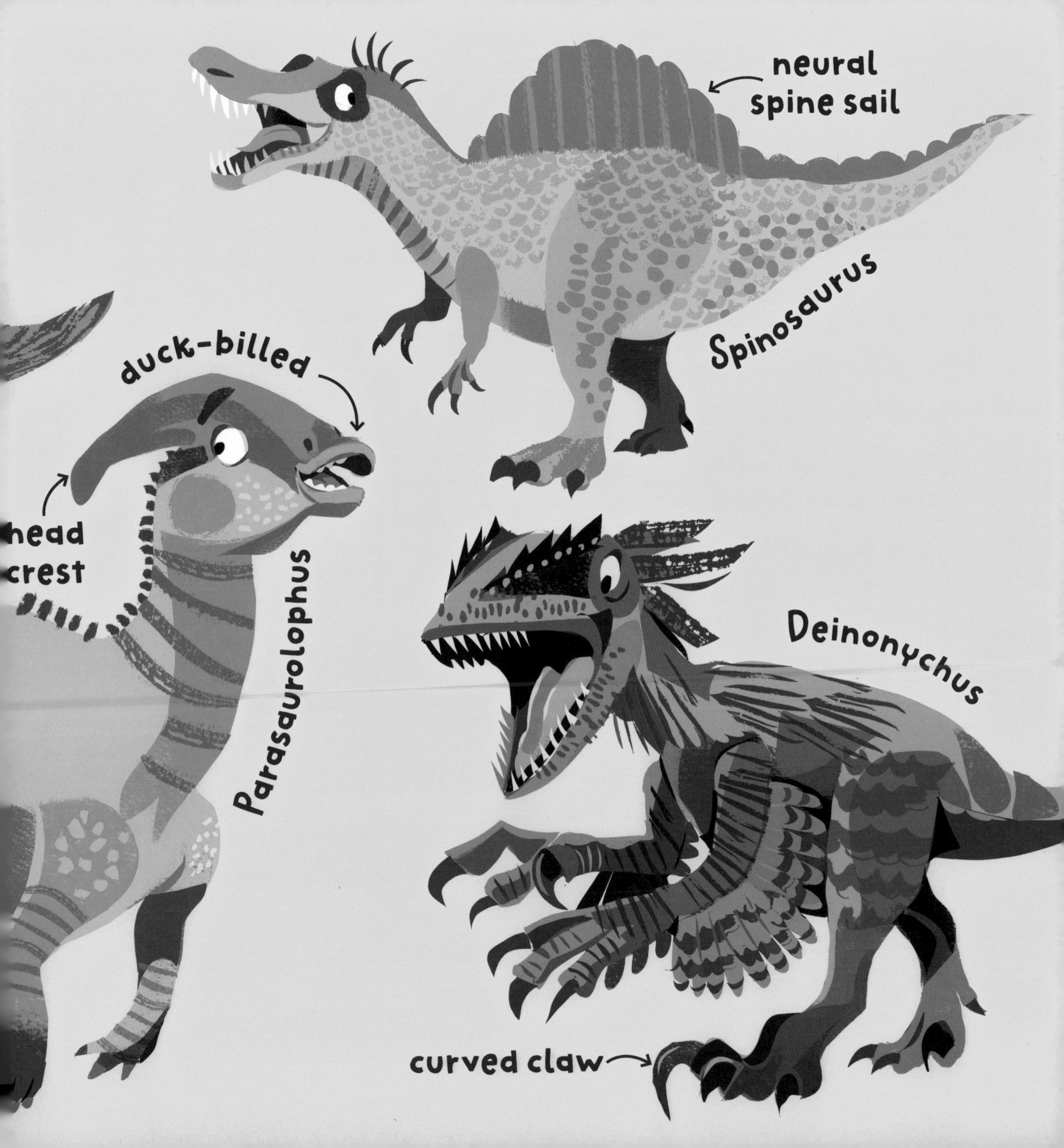
neural
spine sail
Spinosaurus
duck-billed
head
crest
Parasaurolophus
Deinonychus
curved claw

gliding wings
Microraptor
bony plates
Ankylosaurus

tail club
Diplodocus
Some dinosaurs were smaller than a chicken, others were bigger than buses!
Velociraptor

Maiasaura
The name Maiasaura means 'good **mother** lizard'.
dino eggs
ring-shaped nest

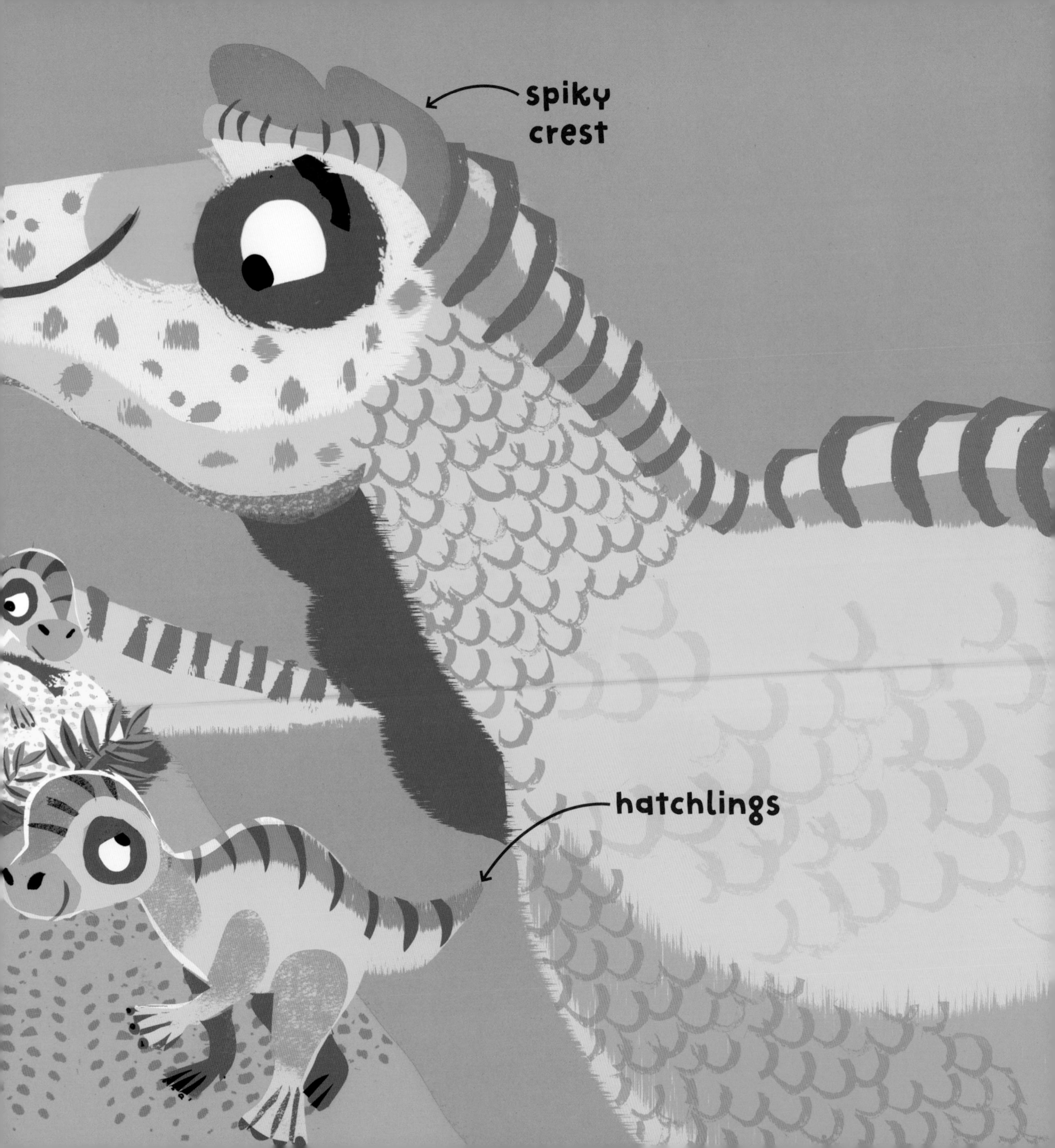
spiky
crest
hatchlings

Fossils take thousands and sometimes millions of years to form.

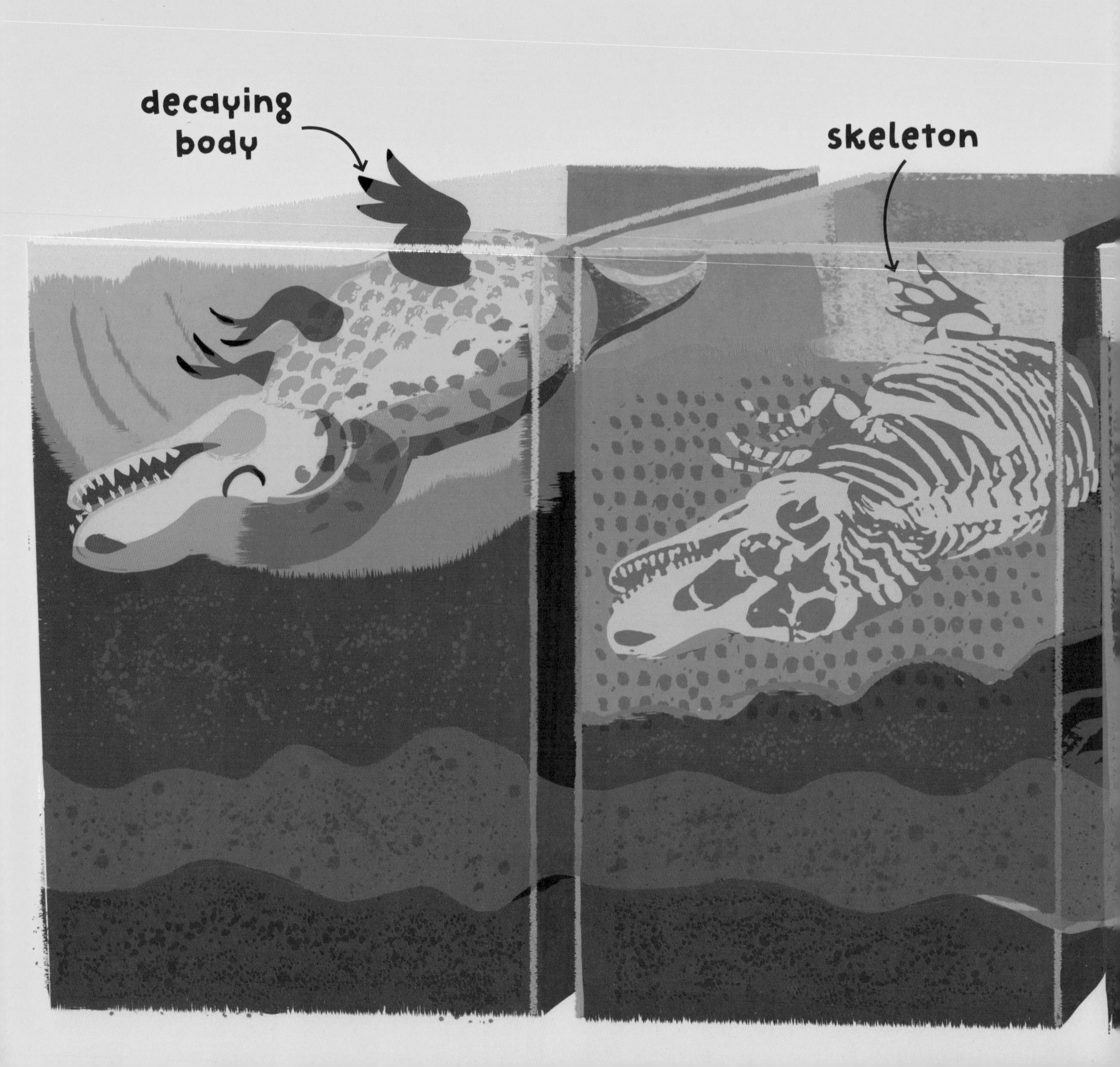

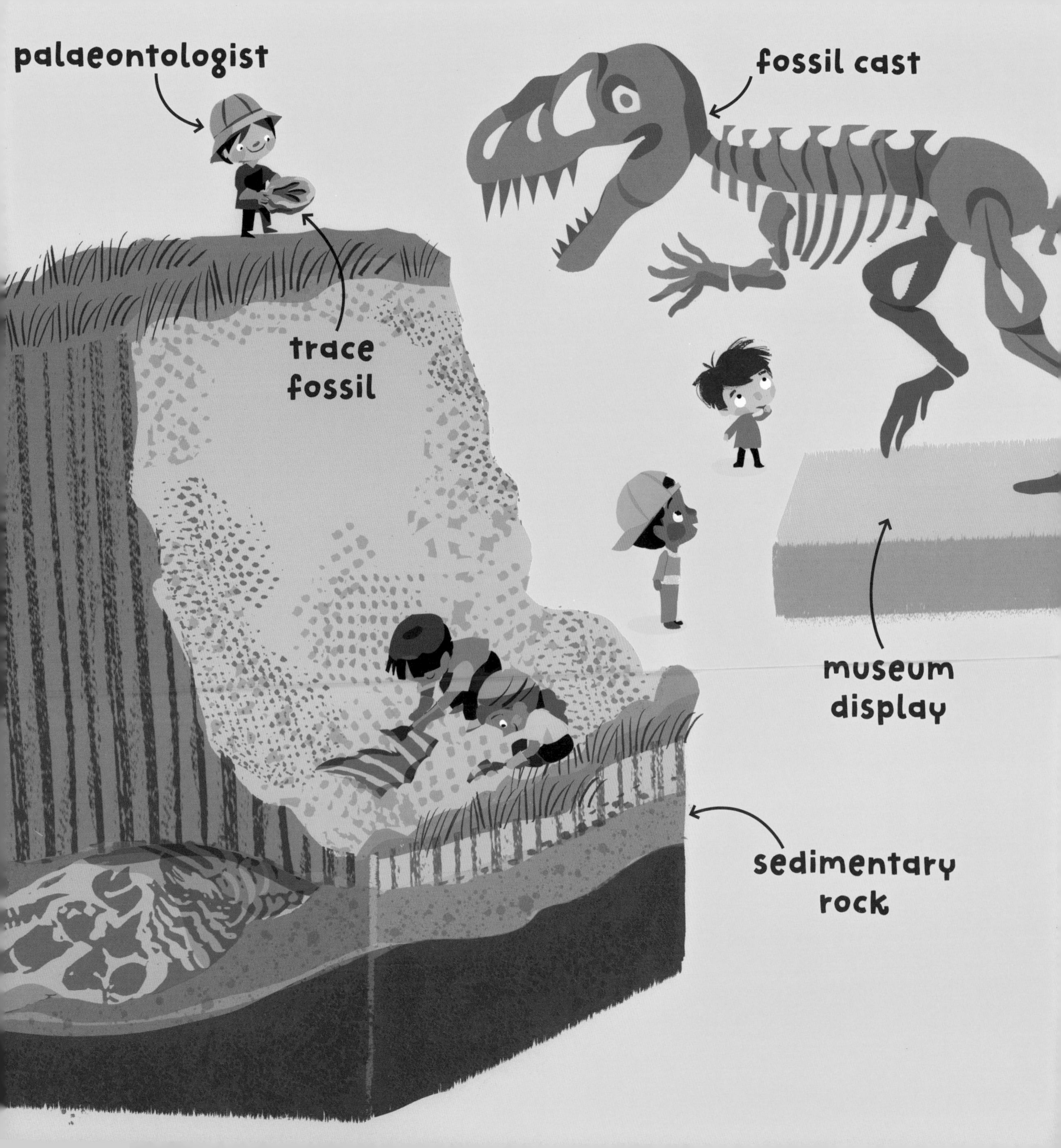
palaeontologist
fossil cast
trace
fossil
museum
display
sedimentary
rock

How to **pronounce** the names (as they appear in the book):

Caudipteryx	caw-DIP-ter-iks
Allosaurus	AL-oh-SORE-us
Tyrannosaurus rex	tie-RAN-oh-sore-us rex
Stegosaurus	STEG-oh-SORE-us
Triceratops	tri-SERRA-tops
Apatosaurus	a-PAT-oh-sore-us
Nigersaurus	nai-ja-SORE-us
Pteranodon	te-RAN-oh-don
Nemicolopterus	NEM-ee-kol-OPT-er-us
Quetzalcoatlus	ket-zal-KWAT-luss
Liopleurodon	LIE-oh-PLUR-a-don
Ophthalmosaurus	op-THAL-mo-SORE-us
Elasmosaurus	el-lazz-mo-SORE-us
Iguanodon	ig-WHA-noh-don
Therizinosaurus	thera-ZINA-SORE-us
Spinosaurus	SPY-noh-SORE-us
Parasaurolophus	para-sore-ROL-oh-fus
Deinonychus	di-NON-ee-kus
Microraptor	MY-crow-RAP-tor
Ankylosaurus	an-KIE-lo-sore-us
Diplodocus	DIP-lo-DOKE-us
Velociraptor	ve-LOSS-ee-RAP-tor
Maiasaura	my-a-SORE-a